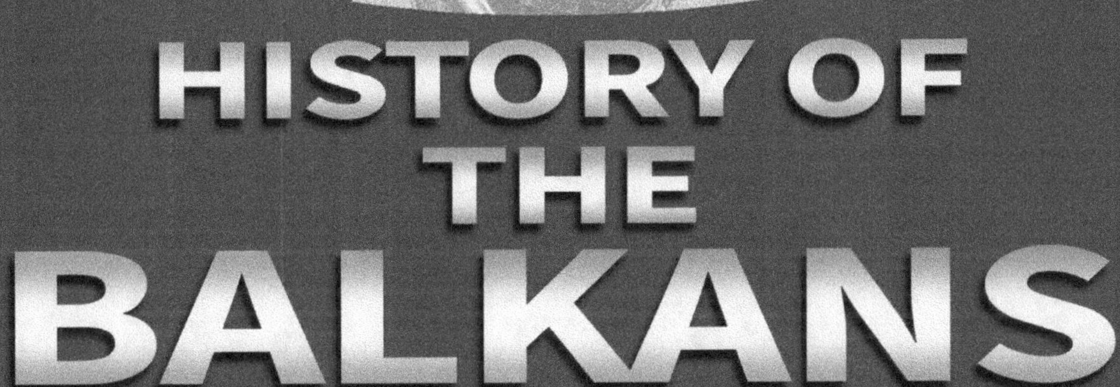

HISTORY OF THE BALKANS

A BRIEF OVERVIEW FROM BEGINNING TO END

HISTORY SHORTS

Bonus Downloads

Get Free Books with **<u>Any Purchase</u>** *History Hub*

Every purchase comes with a FREE download!

History of the Balkans

A Brief History from Beginning to the End

History Shorts

CONTENTS

Chapter One
Introduction

When someone says history, more often than not, a lot of people would think of war, culture, and religion. The Balkans' history is no exception to this thinking. The people in the Balkan peninsula experienced all these, but not in a peaceful way. From the get-go, they were at a disadvantage geographically. While most places can rely on their terrain for protection, the Balkan peninsula had no such privilege. This makes them an easy target for invaders. And as you read through this, you will see that many of the invaders took advantage of their lack of terrain protection.

Before the invaders came, there were different groups and regions in the Balkan peninsula. These cultural groups and areas were divided geographically: the Eastern Balkan, the Central Balkan, and the Western Balkan. These groups and regions helped historians to identify the origins of the people who lived in the Balkan peninsula.

The first invaders that came were the Greeks, who were followed closely by the Romans. The Greeks came in peacefully, but the Romans took the Balkan lands for themselves to conquer. The Romans were able to keep their hold of the Balkan peninsula for a lot longer than the Greeks. However, it came with a lot of resistance, not just from the Balkans but also from the other countries who wanted to claim the Balkan peninsula for themselves. An example of this would be the Byzantine Empire.

The Byzantine Empire held its own for more centuries than the Romans did. Of course, they still had enemies from the inside and outside. Internally, they were ruling with an iron fist, but their rule still had some inconsistencies. Externally, they were threatened by a number of empires like the Bulgarians and the Ottoman Turks.

The next to invade the Balkan peninsula were the Ottoman Turks. These people are responsible for bringing in Islam to the land. But you should know that this was not an Islamic crusade. The Ottomans never intended to claim the Balkan peninsula for their religion, even though, in the end, they did bring it in and tried to spread their faith throughout the land. At one point, Islam and Christianity stood in the peninsula, but not peacefully.

During the Ottoman Rule, there was the 1908 Revolution wherein the sense of nationalism started to overtake the Balkan people. Then the Balkan wars followed this revolution, and this is where the line between civilians and militia was too blurred. Civilian causalities were too high, and the land was in chaos.

But it didn't end there because after the Ottoman Rule came to the world wars. However, the Balkans did have a breath of air for a few years. During the world wars, they were forced to be a part of it, even though they tried their best not to.

Listing down everything, you might feel sorry for the people in the Balkan peninsula because their history is just one country conquering them after another. And they were very divided internally as well, which is another reason why they were so prone to being ambushed; their lands didn't help them either. This is the sad truth about their history; they were always at a disadvantage.

But on the bright side, the Balkan peninsula finally seemed to get its act together towards the end. They were divided at first, but after the World War 2, they appeared to be able to set aside their differences within each other politically and throw away their physical divide due to the landscape of their land to unite as one. Also, through their art, they were able to find their voice and are now making themselves known throughout the entire world. They know that it is time for the world to know that who the Balkan peninsula is; they are ready to put the Balkan peninsula back on the map not as a place to be conquered but as a united country.

Now, their geographical location must be studied to understand why they were so vulnerable and so easily conquered by the Greeks, Romans, Byzantines, and Ottomans. Everything in history has a reason and an origin. And for the Balkan peninsula, that origin is their geographical location.

Chapter Two
Geography

The Balkan peninsula is located in the most eastern part of the three European peninsulas within the Mediterranean area. The other two peninsulas are Italy and Spain, and the terrain surrounding them solidifies their borders. The Balkan peninsula, sadly, has no well-established terrain barrier. However, there is the Danube River, which could be the northern boundary of the peninsula. But having a river as a border is not as great as one may think. Because of the terrain in the Balkan peninsula, internal communication is not easy. This effect is that the Balkan peninsula is divided into many geographic divisions based on its rugged terrain.

Geographers have already acknowledged the Danube River as the northern inland boundary of the Balkan peninsula. By the north of the lower part of the Danube, there is a fertile Rumanian land that has become an important part of the Balkan Peninsula. Besides its waters and rough terrain, the place is also known for its mountain range. The mountains can be divided into three equal sections. The central section is the one with the highest point. The eastern area, also known as Lesser Balkans, is made out of rounded and richly wooded peaks. The western section includes the Balkan passes: Shipka pass, Baba Konak pass, and Isker Valley pass. For the Balkan peninsula, it is really easy to pass into their land.

The people in the Balkan peninsula created roads to help their predicament in internal communication, political purposes, and more. One of the first roads made was the Europe-Asia route; it runs from the northwest to southeast, basically from Belgrad to Constantinople. This road also helped internal communication from the east to the west. Soon enough, these roads or old highways become railroads during the industrial era. Another way the people of the Balkan peninsula tried to fix the internal communication problem was to build harbors. The most important, or the most popular harbors, are Constantinople. Saloniki and Athens. There are also lesser-known harbors: Danubian, Kilia, Sulina, and St. George.

The two climates in the Balkan Peninsula: The Mediterranean and Continental, help with agriculture. Each climate allows a specific type of vegetation. For the part of the peninsula that falls under the Mediterranean climate, the sub-tropical fruits are what flourishes. However, here, meat and bread are limited. For the part of the peninsula that is under the Continental climate, trees grow abundantly. The plains of this region are very green because of it. There are oak forests and valleys everywhere.

The role of the Balkan peninsula in history is determined by its terrain and climate and by its geological location in the different areas. In other words, they were where they were during the wars because of their geographical location.

Chapter Three
The Greek and Roman Epoch

The Greeks time in the Balkan history is roughly around 1500BC to 200BC. The Greeks made their way to the islands of the Aegean Sea and the southern tip of the peninsula, however still within the borders of Hellas. Before the Greeks settled in, they were nomads roaming the grassy plains north of the Danube River. The Greeks slowly made their influence known southward until the extremes of the Balkan peninsula. These ancestors of the Greeks, which we can refer to as the Hellenic nomads, undoubtedly developed a high-end society called the Aegean civilization. These Hellenic nomads took over the agriculture and political system to absorb and adopt it as part of the Aegean influence.

During this time, a group of people lurked by the hills and mountains up north. These people come from the same Indo-European family; however, they do not share the same experiences that the Greeks had on the Mediterranean shores. Although, they do have similarities in barbarism. Nevertheless, they were separated from the Greeks and are now called the Thracians and Illyrians. The Thracians are from the northeast of the peninsula, while the Illyrians are from the northwest. Both call their barbarians as "Macedonians." The Macedonians had the most contact with the Hellenic nomads. They had regular interactions with the Greek settlers, soldiers, and traders.

Most Greeks were merchants, and because of the mountain barriers around the Hellas made traveling so incredibly difficult. This is why they had to trust the maritime merchants. They were able to develop this bond, creating a trading post at the most convenient spot. This post is from the northern shores of the Aegean, past the Dardanelles and Bosporus, and all the way to the Black Sea. The Greek trading posts were scattered around the west coast.

The Roman Epoch of the Balkan history followed right after the fall of Greece. It started when the Romans followed in the footsteps of the Macedonia kingdom. The Romans took their time before striking and conquering them. The ancient Hellas was now made into a Roman province. For Romans to secure their hold, they built a network of highways and military garrisons. Because of this, Dyrrachium came to be. The Romans quickly made cities on the travel lines: of Adrianople, Philippopolis, Sardica (Sofia), Naissus (Nish), and Singidunum (Belgrad). For the Romans to protect what they've got in the Balkan peninsula, they made garrison towns, making a number of river forts from Belgrad to the Black Sea.

Once they secured the military, the politics followed. Roman justice was now in the courts, and it gave their people security. Traders from Italy and other Mediterranean centers came pouring into the city. They settled as local merchants to help with the trade within the garrisons. Soon enough, the people adopted Roman art and culture. Rome's system was considered the highest caliber at the emperor's peak power.

Christianity is one of the most important gifts the Romans brought into the Balkan peninsula. It was easy for the Romans to get the Balkans to transition to Christianity. This shows how weak the people's pagan ways are.

To understand the reasons why the fall of the Roman Empire came to be, remember that the two centuries after the reign of Augustus were the centuries of the Christian era, which was the pinnacle of Roman power. During this time, people didn't dare challenge Rome's authority. In the mainland, emperors were just and fair. The army fulfilled its duties without corruption, and the merchants were civil and peaceful.

However, there was a sudden shift in the peace. The slow disturbance of the machinery of the government and the growing social chaos happened at the same time. This caused the third century of Roman rule to become their century of downfall. The different parts of the army created rivals with some emperors, and they gave no mercy to each other. Then Diocletian tried to turn the tide by changing the political system that and changed it to oriental despotism, meaning that they were now in an absolute monarchy set-up. However, it was a fruitless attempt to save the Empire.

But the decline of government machinery and the start of social chaos weren't the only reason why Roman Empire declined. Another reason is that they started a fight with the Germanic Barbarians. The barbarians may have lost if Rome wasn't crumbling. After all, they were at a disadvantage because they had little armor and not as many fighters compared to the Romans.

Emperor Trajan found himself in trouble because of the chaos by the Danube River. People called the Dacians started crossing the river to steal from the people in the Balkan provinces. These people were not from Germany; however, they were relatives of the Thracians. They attacked because of the Dacians were scared of being colonized by the Romans.

Nevertheless, Trajan sent out people to fight the Dacians and pushed them all the way to the valleys of the Carpathian Mountains. Later on, they named the newly formed province as "Dacia."

News spread when they found out how weak Rome was. The Barbarians weren't the only ones challenging Rome now. People by the borders decided to attack as well. One of the different groups of people fighting Rome is the Mongolians of central Asia. This continuous line of attacks was later called the Great Migrations. A German tribe known as the Goths attacked Dacia. The Romans, who were again weak, retreated to the south of the river. Dacia was the first Roman province to fall to the Barbarians.

The Goths didn't stop there. They continued to cause havoc by the Danubian frontier, and then later, one moved to the Asiatic frontier. Besides the Goths, the Persians were slowly rising to power and making enemies with the Sassanians. This war between the two was too near the Roman provinces in Western Asia. Diocletian went up north to Nicomedia in Asia Minor while Constantine stayed to fight. Constantine made the capitals beautiful. He called the city New Rome, or what we call now Constantinople, and now that is the new capital of the Empire.

The Roman Empire still had difficulty holding down the frontiers. The Balkan peninsula suffered years of chaos because of the continuous waves of war by the Goths, the Huns, the Avars, the Slavs, the Bulgars, the Magyars or Hungarians, the Pechenegs, the Cumans, and the Mongols.

Most of the invaders ran out of their original homelands, so they went to the Roman lands to find a new settlement because of the Romans' wealth. However, the Huns and the Mongols were just raiders and not invaders. The Slavs, Magyars, and Bulgars, however, created settlements.

As the Roman Epoch in the history of the Balkan peninsula declined, the Byzantine Epoch started to rise.

Chapter Four
History After the Greeks and Romans

At the height of the Byzantine empire, it was simultaneously the most powerful empire in the Western world. They had wealth because of trade and prosperous lands. The military was at its peak, having the best weapons they could have at that time. The government wasn't corrupt either; they even adopted a system called "Byzantine diplomacy." And, of course, the reason for the empire's success is that they gave the Balkan people a seat with the powerful. The Balkan rulers hoped to become Byzantine autocrats. During this time, the medieval Balkan civilization became the essence of Byzantine.

However, even though the Byzantine empire made great progress, their fortune was still inconsistent. For example, Justinian tried to fix the empire during the aftermath of the barbarian invasions. Although he tried, he could not find solutions to all the problems they inherited from the Romans. They had struggles in protecting and controlling land. However, the Byzantine empire's chief danger was that their enemies continued to attack from all sides of the peninsula. Even though they defeated the Arabian invaders, many more invaders still tried to claim the Balkan peninsula.

In the sixth or seventh century, the Slavs, an Indo-European people, were able to cross the Danube line and took control of most of the Balkan peninsula. The Slavs had no formal political organization like most groups; however, they still had a strong internal relationship with each other. The Slavs, unlike most invaders, actually settled in the land they conquered. Even though they could reach the gates of Constantinople, they were unsuccessful in defeating it. After this battle, the Byzantine state recovered and gained back its stolen territory.

The Bulgarians were the biggest threat to the Byzantium empire in the Balkan peninsula. They were originally known as the Bulgars, a Turanian people who first settled in the area between the Sea of Azov and Kuban. They were forced out of their homes by the Khazars. Under the leadership of Asparukh, they migrated to the place near the mouth of the Danube. The Byzantine government saw this and let them become an independent state.

Khan Krum, the ruler of the Bulgarians, then expanded their territory. They were able to take possession of the lands from the Slavs. Initially, the Slavs and Bulgarians lived together, the Bulgarians comprising their upper social class.

The byzantine empire sent out Cyril and Methodius to the Greater Moravian Kingdom to ask for help to fight the Roman missionaries. However, they died, and their efforts died with them.

The Bulgarian Empire still was drawn to Byzantium and Constantinople. Simeon, the ruler of Bulgaria at that time, had a primary goal during his reign to be the supreme ruler of the Christian world. Even though he failed many times, he still was able to proclaim himself as the ruler of the Romans and Bulgars. This led to Bulgaria being the most powerful of all Balkan powers.

However, these conquests created internal problems for the Bulgarian leaders. Nobility challenged the main leaders, different religions divided the people, and heresy was rampant. But the internal problems weren't the only issues; they also had external threats. The Byzantine Empire was still their biggest problem. However, the Hungarians and the Pechenegs added to their problems. The Byzantine Empire was on the road to recovery, and the Russians were closing in as well. At first, the Russians claimed the lands of Bulgaria but soon after, the Byzantine Empire forced the Russians out, and they claimed Bulgaria for themselves. Basil II, also known as the "Bulgar Killer," took fourteen thousand Bulgarians and sent them off to battle but not before blinding them in one eye. Afterward, the Byzantine army succeeded in conquering Ohrid, and now the Byzantium was the strongest empire at that time.

The Byzantine Empire, however, could not retain its power. Their territory slowly dwindled, and their internal and political conflicts hurt them. They now have new enemies, the Seljuk Turks and the Hungarians, who are threatening the city through their borders. Because of this, the Bulgarians, taking advantage of the troubles, created a second empire. Constantinople was soon destroyed because of the fourth crusade; this crusade took the wealth for themselves. Soon enough, the Bulgarians came back to power.

Chapter Five
East Balkan Region

The first group in the East was known as the Insula Banului group. They are most known for their pottery skills, and their main designs were the use of ripples, but they used stamped decorations as well. Themes of their pottery are circles linked by tangents put together either horizontally or vertically. Their pottery designs can link this group to the Urnfield culture during the Iron Age I in southern Pannonia and the Gava group, which is northwest of Romania. The other designs link them to the Dubavac-Zuto Brdo group in south Banat.

The next group is named the Badadag group, which was settled by the shores of Bagadag lake. According to historical findings, they dwell in inputs, but houses were still found on the surface made out of wattle and daub. They are also known for their pottery forms, and their work resembles those of the Insula Banului group. They have similar themes, but the difference is they have Fishbone motifs as well. Their stamped decorations, however, were wheels, which is significant because it shows they were there during the late Badadag phase. This shows links to the media group in Romania. Because there were no cultures before them in the Dobruja, historians believe that this group was a descendant of the Insula Banului group.

The last group discussed in this region is the Psenicevo group, which is closely related to the Babadag group. This group settled themselves by the river terraces, specifically between two small rivers. Again, this group is known for their pottery which resembles the Babadag group.

Chapter Six
Central Balkan Region

The Mediana group settled themselves in the Mediana site by Brzi Brod, which is based on a hill. This group had an abundant supply of animal bones which shows that cattle breeding for them was very important in their culture. There are three phases in the life of Mediana, which runs so smoothly that historians believe there was actual inner evolution.

The Donja Brnjica-Gorhja Strazava group is found because of their graves in the southern Morava region and the Kosvoco area in the latter days of Iron Age I. This group was identified using their cemeteries. Studies show that their dead were cremated, and their ashes are in an urn sealed by a stone slab. There were also communal graves, not just individual ones.

The Gave group's archeological evidence was found in the area of River Cris in Romania and Hungary. This group was identified through their biconical urns. Through the study of the urns, historians dated their origins back to the Iron Age I. These urns were also found in southern Pannonia and the southern Morava region.

Are You Enjoying Reading?

As an independent publisher

with a tiny marketing budget

we rely on readers, like you.

If you're receiving help from this book,

would you please take a moment to write a brief review?

We really appreciate it.

Chapter Seven
West Balkan Region

The Western Serbia and the Glasinac Complex are linked to the Illyrian region because of archeological characteristics. Their custom of burying under tumuli was introduced during the Bronze Age's beginning. There is also an uninterrupted cultural evolution seen in this group, especially the Glasinac group nearing the Iron Age IV.

The South Bosnian Region and the Pod grandina is a region of the Balkan peninsula. The South Bosnian group's special characteristic is its very own culture because of its gradinas. The best way to characterize this group is the gradinas at Varvara, which is located on a steep rock, protected on one side by its natural terrain and on the other side by a wall. It is hard to determine this group's origin, but the historians can only roughly guess.

The Dalmatian Region is characterized by its linguistics and its strong connection with Pannonia. However, the start of this connection can't be determined because they don't have the evidence to study it. Gradings are also found in this region. Because of the simple geographical area of this region, it is assumed that they had a closed economic and social unit. Burials under tumulis are also found in this region. There were skeletons placed in a cist; there were flat graves with cists as well. They also have pottery and other metal objects that help place where they are in the period of evolution. The different regions here are the Iapodes and Liburnian.

Chapter Eight
Introduction to Slavic Christianity

Christianity in the Balkan peninsula can be traced back to the earliest apostolic times. It started when St. Paul had a vision of a man who asked for his help and to come over to Macedonia. In the scripture, Paul stated that he preached the gospel to Illyricum, Titus went to Dalmatia, and Demas went to Thessalonica. People continued preaching Christianity, which was why the Illyrian, Thracian and Hellenic people were what they were back then. The preaching of Christianity did not occur to the apostles that it would invite bad consequences.

The number of martyrs in the Roman Danubian provinces during the Diocletian persecution is the reason why Christianity had so much power at that time. There was a string of persecutions of Christians in Dalmatia. One of the people persecuted was Domino, a local bishop. Another persecution was similar to those before in Durostorum in Moesia Inferior.

However, the Balkan provinces were able to have a number of good Christian leaders, such as Jerome. Jerome was born in the area of Dalmatia and Pannonia. There was also Bishop Nicetas of Remesiana in Dacia

Mediterranean and the Arian bishops: Auxentius of Durostorum, Palladius of Ratiara in Dacia Pipensis, and Ursacius of Singidunum. Also, the emperors Constantine the Great, Jovian, Gratian, and the Valentinians were natives of Danubian provinces.

The road of Christianity in the Balkan peninsula wasn't anything but peaceful. This is because the land was a battleground of different invaders, such as the Barbarians and the Romans. Another challenge was that the barbarians who conquered the peninsula were caught in a battle between the Latin and Hellenistic cultures. This caused them to skid off the path of Christianity.

The demise of the Greco-Roman civilization in the Balkan peninsula started with the invasion of the Visigoths. Later on, the Ostrogoths conquered the Dalmatian littoral, and they held it for forty years. However, even with Arianism, there was still room for social and religious organizations. The archbishop of Salona used this to gain authority over the land. Emperor Justinian, who was determined to assert his authority, started a battle with the Ostrogoths. They created an alliance with the Barbarians from the Slavs tribes in an effort to continue the fight with Justinian's army. Even with the help, the

Ostrogoths were defeated, and the Roman's influence was, for that time, revived.

However, the Slavs still was able to put an end to the Greco-Roman civilization, both political and religious, in the Balkan peninsula. This made way for Slavic paganism to become the dominant religion in the peninsula.

For the religious evolution of the Slavs, they never went through animism, ancestor worship, or even basic polytheism. However, when they accepted Christianity, it was implied that the legal and political systems the religion has come with were Byzantine. A lot of the Slavic tribes thought Christianity led to a political problem. This caused some issues with the transition. However, Christianity still succeeded. Even though they accepted Christianity for some material advantages, they considered the Christian beliefs a new form of their own beliefs. For example, their pagan gods were converted into Christian saints. Almost all the pagan traditions and customs of the Slavs were retained in a way since they were slightly changed or adapted. However, at that time, the leaders of Constantinople wanted to make sure all their subjects, including the provinces of the Slavs, were fully Christianized. Therefore, the pagan Slavs' territory became another land for missionaries to go to. However, they did not succeed, and the church had to relinquish all its claim of the region.

The biggest motivation for the Christianization of the Slavic population came in because of the two Greek brothers: Cyril and Methodius, who are known as the "apostles of the Slavs." They were sent by Emperor Michael III and Patriarch Photius of Constantinople to go to Moravia because of Rastislav's request. The brothers preached the gospel to his people in a language the Moravians and the Slovenes understood. In a way, this process of Christianization set up the rise of the native Slavic Christian church.

Chapter Nine
Introduction to Islam

It was easy for the Ottomans to invade the Balkan peninsula because it was so divided. During the fourteenth century, the Balkans were made up of a number of small kingdoms and independent rulers. The Byzantine state occupied Thrace, Thessaly, and Macedonia. The Venetians had Morea. The Bulgarians had been split into three kingdoms: Tarnovo, Vidin, and Kalliakra. Albania had four autonomous leaders. The Serb, Croatian and Bosnian kingdoms were located in the west of the Balkan peninsula. However, they were also in a divided due to political struggles. There was no unity, which was why the Ottomans were able to invade and conquer the whole peninsula.

The Ottomans' arrival to the Balkan peninsula marked the beginning of Muslim conversion. They were Muslim, after all, and they were able to systematically rule the majority of the Balkan peninsula; they ruled for more than five centuries. During this time the fall of Constantinople happened in 1453 because of the forced conversion to Islam.

However, even though the Ottoman conquest happened in the Balkan peninsula, the conversion to Islam was not as successful as one might think.

After the defeat, the continuation of the conversion to Muslim still continued, even though the change was not as drastic as the conversion in Asia Minor. The role of Muslim colonization played a big part in the spread of Islam in the Balkan peninsula during the early stages of Islamization.

There are two parts to the conversion process: the innovator period and the early adopter's period. But as time goes on, there is a third stage in the conversion process, called the early majority period. The pace of the conversion had got faster in the 1649s. It was mostly in rural lands where the conversion took place. During this third period, the conversion of Christianity to Islam stopped in the majority of the Balkan lands. However, it was still continuing in the outer areas.

In the nineteenth century, the conversion from Christianity to Islam in the Balkan peninsula grew inconsistent due to the demographics of the land. But soon enough, the Balkan peninsula has become an Islam land.

In the end, Islam spread both through force and peaceful means. During the first phase of the conversion to Islam, it was more encouraged gently. However, in the second phase, the conversion caused a war, even though towards the end, the Islamic teachings were then combined with the culture of the non-Muslims so that they could embrace the Islam religion.

The fact that there was Christianity and Islam thrived in the Balkan peninsula at one point poses a philosophical problem. This is so because each religion believes that it is the one true faith; each believes that it is the right one and everyone should follow it. Balkanian Islam came to be during the Osman empire because it was during this time that the Christian culture and faith managed to share a place with the incoming Islam culture. This type of Islam has adapted to the Balkan beliefs and created this branch of the Islam faith.

Chapter Ten
Historical Politics (1856-1878)

The countries Great Britain, France, Austria, Prussia, and Russia were Belgium's defense. Still, Britain, France, and Russia were Greece's defense as well. The Congress of Paris in 1856, also known as the Treaty of Paris, is what ended the Crimean War (a battle between the Russians, British, French, and Ottoman Turks). This treaty brought the Balkan peninsula into the ranks of these countries, approved by the Concert of Europe (the preliminary agreement among European monarchies helping them decide on territories and politics for each country).

After twenty years, the Concert, however not entirely gone, was in its decline. At this time, Prussia and Piedmont were in charge of uniting Germany and Italy. Austria and Russia were hit with the conspiracy and rebellion from the Hungarian and Polish nobility. The South Slav, Hellenic and Romanian nationalists were excited about the movement of Italian unification. France, which was under Napoleon III's rule, was ready to support this movement because of its ideology and prestige. The Second Empire became a member of the Concert of Europe. Russia supported the Second Empire because its leaders believed it was the only way to gain back the influence it had lost over the Balkans.

However, Russia did not have a ruling over the Balkans. The time after the Polish insurrection in the year 1863, the Russian's relationship with France was amicable as they turned their hostility to Prussia instead. However, Austria held the record for being a consistent power figure, trying to keep balance and intervening when necessary. The Balkan peninsula during the 1860s was the center of activity for the Italian, Hungarian and Polish nationalists, Russian pan-Slavists, and Italian, French, and Prussian diplomats. All of these people hoped that this would create a way for them to attain their respective goals. All of them were in contact with the government and movements of the Balkans. They had this chance in 1866, but it wasn't pursued because the Balkans were not ready.

Even though they weren't ready, the Balkans started to take matters into their own hands. They've begun diplomacy and changing international protectorates to suit their needs. By taking political actions, they've sent out a signal to the other countries that they are no longer a place to conquer. They started doing activities on their own through their rulers and political groups.

The Balkan states were striving to act still as if they were alone, letting their rulers pattern themselves to the Europeans and forming alliances with them. There were agreements around the Greco-Serbian alliance back in 1867, where they have agreed to participate in the preparations for the uprising of the Ottoman Empire. There were military preparations and a set of strategized diplomatic moves. They did all they could to prepare themselves for this new threat.

The new states were the ones to legalize the rebellions and revolutions. Although the government establishments in villages divided the peasants from the city and state, the monarch and oligarchy had to compete for the support of the peasants. This is the reason why in more democratic societies, the Ottomans were able to conquer them.

Chapter Eleven
Ottoman Rule Over the Balkans

The Balkan society was where the nobility tried converting themselves from a closed estate to one that has opened itself to foreign merchants, sacrificing the peasants to do so. This gave way for the Turks to see that the Balkans had better land than they did. So, with a great militia behind them, they pressed on to conquer the Balkans at a gradual pace.

The first period of this conquest was when the Ottomans wanted people to see that they now had the inheritance left to them by the Eastern Roman Empire and could tolerate the Jews and Christians. When Constantinople's fall was near, the emperor at that time was ready to allow for the union of politics and the Church under the pope. Because of the union, an Emperor is nothing more than just a plain figurehead. However, the patriarch stayed religious even under the Ottoman rule.

The Orthodox Church was the people who believed in that the Christian Roman Empire should be the ruler of the world. Their emperor would represent God on the Earth; he would be bound by politics, the church rules, and the public's needs and wants. Due to the Greco-Roman tradition in their legal matters, there was no need for a monolithic church organization. The bishop of the Church was at the top of the hierarchy.

During the Ottoman rule, they prioritized defending their sources of wealth and maintaining the peace between the social classes and the religious groups. An example of how they were able to do this was that part of their tenurial system was to supply the cavalry.

The Ottomans liked to live in towns where they could you the fertile lowlands as estates. So, they stayed in the eastern and Balkan central cities. During their rule, they made the people in those towns move to another place so their armies could stay in their old lands; this migration was completed for political reasons. Some people started to leave and go beyond the Save and Danube border as refugees. The Turks tried to bring back the people by offering privileges to restore the economy and the land's defenses.

As time passed, the Ottoman Empire became the largest Muslim state. However, the majority of their people in European lands were still Christians. These Muslims belong to the mainstream Sunni branch of Islam, which means they follow the Hannafite Interpretation of the Koranic Law. In the Balkan peninsula, Islam became the leading religion; they would have Christians and Muslims living in one place.

During this time, Christians and Jews were treated differently, and it was politically right; they were fortunate enough to be able to practice their religious customs; however, there were strict restrictions. The Christian and Jewish leaders were part of the hierarchy of the empire. They proved themselves useful when it came to implementing government policies. Coming to the end of the fifteenth century, the spread of Islam affected Bulgaria, Albania, and Bosnia.

Chapter Twelve
Wars

1908 Revolution

The 1908 Revolution was the catalyst for the spread of nationalization of the masses because, during this time, the Ottoman society's mass politics were greatly changed. The rise in the number of people in journalism and civil organizations went up radically, which contributed to the nationalization of Muslim societies. It also affected the ethnic and religious relations between the communities under the empire. The call for the people in the society to be nationalists became a requirement in the lives of the political people. Wars started because there was a need to construct national identities. The Balkan wars are one of the prime examples of this.

Balkan Wars and Total War

The countries of Greece, Serbia, Montenegro, and Bulgaria, who were able to regain their independence from the Ottoman empire, declared war on the same Empire in 1912. The diverse religious and ethnic groups that are within the Balkan peninsula incited a power struggle between the Balkans and the Great Powers (the countries China, Russia, France, United Kingdom, and the

United States). Even though the Ottoman militia was eventually defeated and they lost their hold on most of the Balkan lands, competition rose among the rival nationalism and nation-states that started another conflict.

The Ottoman Empire regained its old Capital, Edirne, during the Second Balkan War in 1913. The armies went back and forth; the aggressive states' ethnic cleansing politics were done in the regions. Even though the Empire was able to regain its power over some lands, it took a great hit because of the 1908 Revolution. The Balkan wars were an important turning point in Turkey's history because it was a catastrophe and a disgrace among the political elite.

Because of the Balkan Wars, there was a change in the structure of war in the nineteenth century. An example of this would be the Total War, where the line between militia and civilians was gone. The ones at the center of the wars tried to involve the Great Powers and their own people to join the fight. However, the war battles didn't remain on the battlefield but also turned politics into a battleground. Everything that has happened took a toll on civilian life.

The Balkan civilians weren't the only ones affected by their own war; the other countries were affected too. In turn, the civilian population became a resource to be used during this time. Both sides wanted to weaken the other's population and force their own people to take a more active role in the war.

During the twentieth century, atrocity propaganda became its own battlefield, making it a weapon to undermine the enemy. In the Balkan states, atrocity propaganda caused the stigmatization of the local enemies. On the hundredth anniversary of the Balkan wars, this type of propaganda was used against the Muslims who tried to defend the Ottoman Empire.

During the Balkan Wars, the Christians were terrorizing the Muslims; there were reports of tortured Muslims who were tortured by the non-Muslims, which caused them to support the Ottoman Empire. Torture wasn't the only way they attacked the Islamic people; they also used the dissemination of periodicals and pamphlets. The Islamic people then rallied against the local Christians, who they saw now as enemies of their country.

While the line between the fighters from the civilians continued to blur, unnecessary civilian casualties reached a new high. In the Balkan Wars, people tried to terrorize the coreligionists into participating in the international and national public opinion. This is now termed as "atrocity propaganda." Clear journalism helped the atrocity propaganda during the wars. Because of the misery the Muslims were feeling, and they lost their territory just before the

Balkans war; it was around the time of the boycott movements against Austria, Bulgaria, and Greece. This movement helped weaken the Ottoman politics during the 1908 Revolution, which made way for the tense relationship of the rival nationalisms.

The Balkan wars were also the turning point for the Turkish nationalism. The final defeat of the Ottoman Turks who fought in the Balkan wars started the political elite's nationalist goals, which gave way to the morbid wars between the different religious communities, whose tensions with each other were already at their peak because of the battles. Atrocity propaganda helped a lot of stigmatization and demonization of the non-Muslim people. There were plenty of stories about the pain the Muslims went through at the hands of the Balkan states. This inspired another goal of the writers of atrocity propaganda; their main purpose is to compile evidence and analyze it to be able to plan their revenge.

Atrocity propaganda's most important purpose in the Ottoman Empire was to create moving feelings for the fighters. The pamphlets lit a fire in the soldiers, inspiring them to keep fighting.

World Wars

No one in the Balkan region wanted to be a part of World War 1, but they had no choice but to face it. They suffered from serious economic problems and mass causalities. In the less-developed societies, the impact of the causalities wasn't boarded off to only the people, but to the animals as well. In the years that followed World War 1, the Balkans were experiencing instability and insecurity. There were political extremists who took advantage of this chaos through mass demobilization and their attempt to regain civilian production. Seeing as the rising order of Russian bolshevism was their main threat, the Balkan states outlawed communist parties from their land at the end of 1925.

During the Great Depression of 1929 – 1932, the Balkan states, as they were produced exporters, took a great hit because of the economic crisis the Great Depression brought. Since the agriculture prices were taking a blow, they had to lower them. The Balkan peasants were caught in "price scissors," which means that there is "a widening gap between the rising costs of imports and the shrinking farm income available to pay for them." But that is not all the Great Depression brought to the Balkans. It also highlighted another issue they had: their population growth. Their population growth rate was too high for a time such as this. How the Balkans responded to the Great Depression can be categorized into three policies: cost reduction, debt alleviation, and market monopolization.

World War 2 brought about drastic changes in the ethnic scope of the Balkan states. In each and every Balkan territory, the Nazis came in. They carried out their "final solution," which was the destruction of the Jewish people. There were some resistance movements in the Balkan regions, but it wasn't consistent. When it ended, thanks to the soviet liberation, the Balkans were again united.

Chapter Thirteen
Current Balkan Art

The public's perception when it comes to social problems is very important. What really makes a social problem is not scientific. Still, it is made from the people's awareness and how their values interact with the situation. There are three social problems are possessing according to the people:

- It is widely thought to be the source of the issues.

- People believe it causes the actions or inactions of the people.

- They think it affects too large a number of people.

Artists are able to find inspiration anywhere without creating a connection between the public and the high class. Also, artists can convey the current social reality through their work. Art is how the artists send a secret and important message to different social groups.

There is a relationship between art and society; the relationship is connected because art expresses how the community is currently doing. Art shows the changes in society, actions, and behaviors. It can hone in on a specific class or a specific action in life; it translates to what moment the artist wants to capture.

Expressionism was rampant in the first part of the twentieth century, for it made itself known as a continuation of elementary art. Still, also it is a liberating, anti-academic vision, trumping the Greek classicism. The countries that showed a lot of expressionism are Spain, Germany, and France. They are all situated in Western Europe, so it was easy to have them share this interest.

Balkan expressionism is usually studied randomly only, even though the land is part of Europe, where expressionism is rampant. Artists summarized the Expressionist movement in five points: One is that art is an expression of yourself, the inner workings, and your own emotions. Two is that this type of art values living without boundaries. Three is that it wants to achieve synthetic forms through synthesis and abstraction. Four is that it has an interest in archaic cultures. And fifth is that it has a nonconformist social attitude and is anti-bourgeois and pacifist.

One of the Balkan artists is Paul Hitter, who was born in 1982. He is a painter, and his art can be said to have similarities to the medieval figures. His works are full of symbols that require a lot of concentration to be able to comprehend what Hitter is trying to say. He was named as the "painting machine" since he gets restless when he has a canvas in front of him.

There are other Balkan artists; there is Eugene Al Pann, a painter as well. Matei Serban, another painter, usually focuses on mural painting. There is Marina Obradovic (who was actually born in France). She is a photographer, a painter, and a decorator.

The Expressionist movement is just starting, and the Balkan expressionism movement is rising and making itself known internationally. They believe they do not deserve to be forgotten now. They have so much to tell from their culture and their history. This is where the Balkan artists get their pride and confidence; they know how rich their story is and are motivated to share them with the world.

Chapter Fourteen
Conclusion

Having read everything, what are your feelings toward the Balkans? Do you feel sad for them because their leaders kept changing due to their huge number of conquerors? It would be expected to feel a bit of sympathy for the people of the Balkan peninsula. After all, their history is full of war and empires trying to take their land from them.

History is always a great lesson. And from acquainting yourself with the history of the Balkans, what lessons have you learned? One of the things you must know by now is that everything in history has a reason and purpose. That is why you must learn everything you can about a topic's history. May it be as simple as the geographical location of a country or as complex as the different eras of history itself, it is all equally important because it will help you understand why things happened the way they did. For example, I'm sure you'll be wondering why so many societies tried and succeeded in conquering the Balkan peninsula IF you didn't know how its borders weren't as defined as the other peninsulas during its time. It is just as simple as that.

After reading, you must also know by now that it is never too late to turn things around. Look at the Balkans, for example. They have been through so much; they have been through many wars and countless invaders, and where are they now? The Balkan peninsula is still here to this present day as a united land. Not only that, from being a land of staying mostly quiet as societies trample on them, they are now vocal through their art, wanting the world to know who they are and what they can do. It is marvelous to see this shift in perspective from them.

Lastly, something that you must also remember about the Balkans and should be able to apply to your current life is that you should not let physical space stop you from being united. You can use this in relationships – and I don't mean just romantic ones. If you are separated from your family because they live in one place and you've moved out to live in a distant place, don't let it destroy your relationship with them. Physical space is just space. This is something the Balkans learned over time. In their history, you would notice that they were divided mostly because of the landscape of their peninsula. But in the end, after the wars, they could set aside that aspect and come together to form a united front.

Remember these takeaways. Remember that everything has a reason, has a purpose. Remember that there is no such thing as "too late to turn things around." Remember never to let physical distance stop you from creating and retaining relationships. Apply all of these to your life, and it will surely be great. And never forget about the Balkans. Because they deserve good attention after everything, they've been through.

Chapter Fifteen

Discussion Question

Because of their terrain, the Balkans were at a disadvantage every time a new invader comes along. And they are aware of this problem. If you were a part of their community, would you find a way to fix this problem to avoid everything that has happened to them? What is your plan?

Discussion Question

There were a number of Balkan invaders. There were the Greeks, the Romans, the Byzantines, and the Ottomans. In your opinion, what conqueror was the best for the Balkan peninsula? Or do you think all of them just destroyed the land?

Discussion Question

The Romans and Slavs helped bring Christianity into the Balkan society. The Ottomans, on the other hand, brought in Islam. Why do you think invaders bring in their religion when conquering a society? Would you force your own religion to other people?

Discussion Question

For a time, Islam and Christianity were living in the Balkan peninsula at the same time. As expected, it was not a peaceful time because they would clash with each other. How would you make these two religions live harmoniously with each other?

Discussion Question

Atrocity Propaganda is when someone spreads information about the actions of an enemy to destroy their reputation. This was used extensively in the wars. Do you think this is a good way to help win a battle? Or is it too small of a contribution?

Discussion Question

During the Balkan wars, there was a blur between the lines of civilians and the soldiers. If you were a political figure during that time and you are seeing this, would you do something about it? Why do you think the lines blurred between them and was it really necessary?

Discussion Question

The Balkans wanted no part in the World Wars and yet they were still involved. Do you think there is a way to not be part of such an integral point in the world's history? Why do you think the Balkans wanted no part?

Discussion Question

Art is a way to express oneself. Why do you think suddenly the Balkan artists

want to come out of the shadows? Do you think it's because of nationalism?

Why or why not?

Chapter Sixteen
Quiz Question

1. **True/False:** The Balkan peninsula had no clear border. However, it had the Danube River. Although, that didn't help much when it came to the invaders.

2. **True/False:** The Greeks and the Romans were the first to invade the Balkan peninsula. The Romans, who were originally nomads, were the ones who invaded first. They were followed quickly by the Greeks.

3. **True/False:** Islam and Christianity co-existed during the Ottoman rule. At first it was a rocky relationship. However, in time, they were able to harmoniously co-exist.

4. **True/False:** The Ottomans brought in the Islam religion. However, they did not do it in a way that were like the Christian crusades. It was more of a "package deal" set up.

5. **True/ False:** The Revolution before the Balkans War happened in 1909. It was a catalyst for the spread of nationalization of the masses. It also happened during the Ottoman Rule.

6. **True/False:** There were two Balkan wars. Both, however, used Atrocity Propaganda. And it also sparked the Total Wars.

7. **True/False:** The Balkans were fortunate enough to only experience the effects of the second world war. They were not affected during the first world war. Also, they did not experience the Great Depression.

8. **True/ False:** The art movement of expressionism was all the rage in Western Europe. The Balkan artist were able to learn this movement as well. They want to use art to show the world who the Balkans are.

Quiz Answer

1. True

2. False: The Greeks were the nomads and the ones who invaded first, not the Romans.

3. False: They never harmoniously co-existed. They were in a constant battle.

4. True

5. False: The revolution happened in 1908.

6. True

7. False: The Balkans experienced both wars and the Great Depression.

8. True

Bibliography

This is a map of the Balkan Peninsula.

The Byzantine Empire's map of their conquests.

This is a mosaic of Bishop Jerome of Dalmatia.

"St Jerome translating" by Lawrence OP is licensed under CC BY-NC-ND 2.0. To view a copy of this license, visit

https://creativecommons.org/licenses/by-nc-nd/2.0/?ref=openverse.

A picture depicting the fall of Constantinople to the Ottoman Turks.

The Ruins of the Balkan Wars (1991)

Names of the fallen Soldiers during the Balkan Wars (1991)

This is a photo of Paul Hitter, a Balkan artist.

Bonus Downloads

*Get Free Books with **<u>Any Purchase</u>** History Hub*

Every purchase comes with a FREE download!

Thank You For Reading

As an independent publisher

with a tiny marketing budget

we rely on readers, like you.

If you're receiving help from this book,

would you please take a moment to write a brief review?

We really appreciate it.